SOME DISTANT PIN OF LIGHT

Francine Witte

Červená Barva Press
Somerville, Massachusetts

Červená Barva Press
P.O. Box 440357
W. Somerville, MA 02144

editor@cervenabarvapress.com
http://www.cervenabarvapress.com

Visit the bookstore at:
http://www.thelostbookshelf.com

Production: Allison O'Keefe

ISBN: 978-1-950063-90-1
LCCN: 2024941448

CONTENTS

A loving thank you to my husband, Mark Larsen,
for his unwavering support of my writing.

SOME DISTANT
PIN OF LIGHT

Map of Me

Let's start by saying this isn't
a map you'd fold up in a glove box
or pull up on a GPS. And maybe
it's not a geography anyone wants
to travel. I mean, hell, somedays,
even I don't. It's just that I started

drawing it one night after too many glasses
of wine, and somebody asking what
I was looking for. He probably meant
in a husband, that loaded question
online dates ask when they are trying

to get laid. I said, there's a part of me
that wants kids, and I labeled that part
the ovaries. Somewhere mid-terrain.
Meanwhile my brain, up north, kept
saying *white carpet, spontaneous sex,*
and other childless things. This went back

and forth until I gave up. Zigzagged
random lines, fake boundaries. And now,
anyone looking at me can see that my borders
are always shifting. If you try to read
this like a real map, it is liable to drive

you into a lake. Meanwhile, my roads
go unpaved, my routes unmarked. I probably
have countries inside of me talking secession.
Rebel leaders planning a coup. Uprisings
even the press is too afraid to cover.
And there I am, just sitting and pouring
myself another glass of wine.

What I Would Tell Adam and Eve

First of all, I'd show up naked and empty
of knowledge. Those two things were never
connected. Tell them to rake up the garden,
clear out the snakes. Shake up the notion that
they were there all along, alongside orchards
plump with apples, perfect and round. Stay calm,
I'd tell them, yes there's a God, but he's not a
life coach, he's not there to keep your kids
from killing each other. And he didn't need
a snake to tempt you. Hunger would have done
that in the end. Finally, I'd tell them both to
enjoy God now before the whole human thing
fans out to seven billion and gets so bad that
even God is afraid to come down from the sky.

First Conversation, Maybe

*So, if the apple won't satisfy your hunger,
what will?* Here, God waits for an answer.
Eve says nothing. A rage begins to build.
Call it wind, call it a hurricane that might
tear the skin off a garden. But no. This is
a patient God, He decides to taste the apple
himself. Rolls the bitterness of knowledge
around on his God tongue and presto! comes
up with names for everything: hurt, disease,
a thousand, thousand more names. Meanwhile,
Eve is standing in the sweet shadow of leaves
waving over her head. The sudden fullness she
feels as she thinks about what will satisfy her
hunger. And she answers God's question, and
her answer again is simple. *Nothing.*

Day Song

Underground thrum, a bass line
mixed with blown-up notes
that form a melody. The sky
is stupid with sun and loves
it, smiles lemon, hums along. Scent
of lilac, vanilla ice cream, sweet maple
air, faint sound of bee buzz feeding
the earth and us. Soft lick of Milk
Duds in the back row of *Cinema V*,
Friday night date, lanky boy hand
reaching bee-like for his date, also
a thrum, and there we are,
all of us singing the day.
We flow lyric each
morning into the open mouth
of another day. Each one of us
a syllable. Each one of us a word.

Our Shadows Met Before We Did

Angle of sun. Physics of how
it lands on the sand. Shadows
stretched and dark. Water lifting
us up. We are weightless. Words
are unseen, but have edges and points.
They are carried to my ear on waves
of sound. Show them to me. Everything
that makes me love you is invisible.

How the Light Hits

The trees are facing north. North
is where you are tonight, thoughts

of me escaping your head like children
at recess. Here I am walking by my own side

down a street where even the moon,
big and whole as it is, can only light one edge

of a forest. That's the thing about being
everywhere. It can't be done.

When you were here, together we were a lightplanet.
We could fan out and shine up the street;

even cat's eyes, sudden emeralds, would emerge
from under parked cars. But now, the moon

does what it can. And who can blame it?
The moon, after all, is only human.

Even in the Shark World

there are rules, laws about
sleep-swimming and razor
teeth and what the sharkbelly
wants. Like my father and
his own rules, laws for his kingdom,
our tiny apartment with the neighbors'
footsteps pattering above, a layer of
interruption between my father
and God. I remember my father
shaking his fist at the ceiling.
Aren't you listening? he would say,
his fish mouth opening and closing
with tired, unheard words.
You just gotta stop.
I was never sure
who he was yelling at,
the neighbors with their
muffled shuffling, or the God
who my father swore was always
testing him. Either way, I wanted him
to let go, let the ocean glide him
forward, be like those sharks
who keep moving even with
speargashes in their skin.
Forget about the neighbors,
forget about God. Remember
only survival, and keep your eyes
fixed on the food fish up ahead of you,
rather than the harpoon boats hovering above you,
that are more likely to get you
if you are standing still.

That Time at Coney Island

Oh, you were there. I saw you.
There was an ocean, hot dogs
and ice cream cones. There
were seagulls who only knew want.
They flew near us. Eyed us, hoping
we would drop scraps. Eye beads
like blackened stones watching
us for one false move, one letting down.
We never gave it to them. Silly birds.
Stop wanting, we almost told them.
You are a bird. You can have bird things.
Pebbles and sandworms or fish that wash up.
And then there was you. Always having
to go somewhere. Always a thing I was
watching. You, about to fade into
the horizon. Me, my eyes like
blackened stones.

If I Turn Animal

all fang-y and hungernose, things might look up. The river wouldn't look as dirty, carrying the sins of upstream, all shit and litter and leftover light from last night's tired moon.

If I turn animal, stretch out long and lean, dig my paws, really plant them into the damp hungry soil, I might start to see the river again as quench and cool, surrender myself to its dark, unanswered question.

If I turn animal, tooth and claw my only words, then maybe the world starts to listen, maybe you start to listen. Maybe a tint of blood from a torn skin colors the water. Maybe the words of a million children start to flow into a million ears.

And maybe the river finally answers its question, going mudless for once, and the hands of the children get filled but stay open and ready for more. And everywhere seeds plump up and burst, and the foot I've been limping on all day toughens up at the heel, steels up around the toes, the whole thing going hooflike, split and sure.

And the mountain in front of me goes flat, like a father's back when he leans down and tells his kid to climb on.

And the river to my right goes gentle, lapping softly like a tongue -- the tongue of an animal settling onto the forest floor, content after a kill.

Go On, Count Your Chickens

All of them. What have you got
to lose? These are not the hard-
boiled, easy-over omelet babies
you've been warned about. These
are not the painted-up ovals
rolling on the neighbor's Easter
lawn. This is a sure thing. Like lust
in the eyes of a smoky stranger
sitting at the end of the bar. These
are eggs under a fat hen mama, warmth
and feather and cluck. It's you nodding
back at that stranger, your mouth forming
that perfect, silent yes, and the falling
flower of your dress later hitting the floor.
Oh sure, you might tap open a shell
now and then, get a beaky surprise.
Or maybe that stranger was eyeing
a woman standing just past your shoulder.
But for now, let's calls the odds in your
favor. Line everything up. Eggs and lust
and just start counting. One chicken, two.
You get it. Just do it. I'll wait.

The River's Wife

Each night, I ask him if he still loves me. He tells me
instead how he started out as a handful of rain, a mountain
stream, how it all grew into a muscled flow. I ask him again
and he goes back to hiss and spin. I give up, head home,
lonely, cutting my feet on scrags of rocks and fallen twigs.

Some nights I wake up, go to the kitchen, turn on the faucet
full blast. Waterfingers lacing my own. My father warned me,
he said the river is made up of tears from all the fish that never
made it out to sea. He said he was a river once, a foaming, raging
twist of a man who lured my mother from the banks. How she

gave up, girl-like, to his tumble and roar. How I, myself,
am part river. How if I listen close enough, I can hear the hiss
and watery spin that is louder than the beating of my heart.

Careful

My mother fluffs up an egg, careful
not to spill it over the sides of a bowl.
Her face, finally unclenched months
after my father's death, a death that
slammed her hard. Came without
a word. Oh yes, there was a word.
Careful. Careful, the doctor said.
Careful, red meat and alcohol said.
To her, it was a word that came and went.
Careful, before a rainfall that either
happened or it didn't. Careful, a broken
condom, the one that made her a mother.
She tells me this one drunken night
when my father was going mid-life,
finding calm in the arms of the neighbor,
the same neighbor who was the first
to bring a casserole after his death. Careful,
my mother, holding back accusation,
because, she said, that's what the civilized
do. Careful. My mother alone now, an egg,
a solitary breakfast. Always an umbrella.
A word not spoken, a bowl she
is careful to stay inside of.

When I Think About Jake

I think of him drop-kicked across the couch,
Freshman dorm. Him coming back from a mixer

where the punch was spun with vodka. He'd
sleep it off, and when he woke, we'd talk to him

for hours, me and Julie, whose baby would end up
having Jake's eyes. Julie would say that Jake's a goof

and everyone knows it, but that didn't stop love from
smacking her in the heart. I wanted to warn her, but

didn't, and six months later, Jake was needle-
dead. Julie would sleep in the scoop on the couch where

Jake had flopped himself so many times. By now, her belly
had swollen into a face. When she tossed and turned,

I could hear her dreams where Jake had his ropey arms
around her, swinging her dosey-doe, the spin of it

getting her passion-drunk. When she woke up, she would
shake her head, throw words like *shame* and *potential*

into the air, let them sail like a football and splat to the floor.
Now, she calls out of nowhere. Twentieth reunion, and do

I want to go? We haven't talked in forever, and she texts
me a photo of her son, grown now, with Jake's gangly arms,

only trackless. I think how sometimes the past can be fun,
only not when it's a sick I finally got cured of. Not with

the echoes of what I should have told her, and told her again
if she didn't hear it the first time. Walk away from it, another

echo is saying, only this time it's for me. It's for Julie.
And even, in a way, for Jake, whose ghost still hovers

above us all, an invisible hand ready to press itself down.

The Year of You Gone

It was month number five
in the year of you gone. Some

people still called it May. Not
me. I wouldn't give it a name.

It barely deserved a number, though
the whole year circled me in a zero.

Everywhere was sad with daffodils hunched
over like old women, branches scabby

and bare. You would have liked it, this
year of you gone, might have said

it suited me. But you were busy elsewhere,
with your own year, paintbrush of leaves

against a pastel sky. The sun, not a zero
but more of an open yellow mouth filled

with fancy words and promises that would
vanish quick as dandelion puffs blown

into a trusting wind.

Other Summers

We were wolves then, doing
the wander ponder, our hunter

hearts pulling us through the forest
night. We needed to eat adventure

and so, we would nosepush anything
lying still. We would roll it over

and roll it over and when it did move,
even a little, we would tear into its skin,

our teeth and tongues, a hurricane of need,
the only light coming from the moon

and a sash of milkstars. The only sound
the whisper of a wind in our throats

slowing back down to a breath.

The Marsh Fills Up

with animal goo. Residue of breath
and struggle. The news gets worse
each day. All the fish go murky blind,
swim into cabinets of reeds. Somewhere,
another gun, another fire. The fish can't
find their way out. They wait for rescue
that doesn't come. The fish end up
at the boggy bottom, flesh-rot and nothing
but a stand of marsh grass marking
their graves. A town of fish death
that continues to grow. We pile
our hurts in an inside place. They
turn into cities, they turn into worlds.

The Better Way to Go

One minute, an apple is bloating into ripeness,
and the next, it's waiting for one good wind
to knock it to the ground. An apple's life
is short. It goes from seed to plump, to plop,
but that doesn't stop its need to be. It's like
those family dinners that no one understands
but can't give up, where Uncle Hank bumbles
drunk across the couch, where Aunt Lil tucks him
in with the afghan quilt that was never meant
to cover him whole, his long legs dangling
uncovered across the arm rest. He will snore it
off, leaving everyone else to finish dinner,
clinks of glass and plates being scraped,
and when he does wake up, Aunt Lil will insist
he eats something, like she always does, because
this is her answer to everything. And even
though everyone's finished, thinking about
traffic and train schedules home, she is busy
scanning the table, fizzed-out root beer, leftover
ham and lands finally on the fruit bowl. Banana
smiles and kiwi fists and yes, of course, the apple,
which she picks up, easy prey, nothing to peel.
And if an apple has a last thought, maybe,
it's this: which is the better way to go, after all,
to shrivel unnoticed, tossed and forgotten? Or have
Uncle Hank's sour breath, his slurry words
the last thing it ever feels on its skin.

It is 1951

And my father is eyeing my mother like a hungry man. Tonight, after work in the post-war, picket-fence, big tree boom of finally having everything, in the house he will lose soon in a business deal.

But for now it is an night of violins stringing up in the air, and the air is a perfume on the sweet floral of my mother's neck. This is what people do in 1951, in the post-war boom, when there is a room, my room, in the back of the house, a nursery, and it is waiting to be filled.

So, after dinner, my mother's lamb chops still a taste on their tongues, my father pulls her gently into their bedroom, and he pushes aside the bedspread with the tiny pom poms, and guides her down, and he smooths aside her hair, and a low-flying bird has landed on a branch outside the window.

This bird, the color of blackberries, feathers shiny in the light of the lowering sun, may or may not be important. May or may not be saying to not make a child in a room you won't have much longer. Maybe this jump from young and carefree to parent is not a good idea.

The apartment they will have to move to, table wedged into the tiny kitchen, baby with another on the way. Dreams burned up like lamb chops left too long on the stove.

But bigger than that, bigger than fear, than loss, is hope, no, the hope of hope. The pom pom bedspread pushed aside, the whole time, the bird tapping on the window. My father listening instead to violins.

Picasso's Weeping Woman

What was it made her cry like that?
Her face broken into here and over
there? She must have started out an
egg, same as everyone, unfertilized
and calm, until spermshatter starts us
on a life of break and heal

                    break and heal.

                         Last time
she was put back together her edges
didn't match, I guess. But then again
neither do ours. We always go back
different. We call it growth, and use
our tears to soften our faces, our eggs
with eyes and ears that see everything,
hear everything, till one day, deathshatter
ends us, and not even other people's tears
can put us back together again.

Shopping for the Storm

The one that never comes, only
I don't know that now. Right now
I'm stocking up on milk and bread,
gluten and lactose be damned. I hear
the soft snickers of the store clerks
who have seen this all before, the men
hefting sacks of salt like chubby toddlers,
grabbing shovels by their scrawny necks,

only to go home and tuck themselves in,
same as me, wait for the avalanched tumble,
for the storm to snowball into snow. Only
it never does. No one wants it, of course,
but it feels to me like that time I waited
for Joey Goldfarb to call like he promised,
how I went out and bought a new outfit,
got my hair colored for the first time, and
how I never heard from him again. It's funny

that we don't talk about fake weather, but
there it is. The weatherman's face an embarrassed
boulder, snow estimates changing and re-changing.
He is waving his hand across the tri-state map.
Lucky us, he is saying. *The storm went out to sea*,
though we'll never know if that's true. Instead,
I keep looking out my window, the sky, a gray face.
I will wait like I did even after I stopped checking
my phone to see if Joey had called. Meanwhile,
on the TV, the weatherman is shrugging
his mountain shoulders, the slow fade
back to the news.

Direction

Like a bloodcell that only knows its way
to the heart, like waves that only know
how to flow oceanward, like fingernails
that don't know how to stop growing

like doors that only know how to open and close

I follow the same old ache that leads me
lovewards, that takes me always straight
to you, I follow the old scent to you, your
touch, your taste, your direction

but then I remember the emptiness I saw last night in your eyes

and I turn back home for once.

The First Snow

Not of the season, but ever.
Falling, like it did on unmanned

land, sometimes fluttering upwards
in a gentle spin of wind, feathered

and swirled as the first thought which
would come up in a much later snow when

Human appears and thinks *I am a thing,*
later I will have a name and there will be

billions of me. The unthought thought,
of course, is how much clearer the snow

would sound without the thwack of an ax
or the crackle of fire, without the thud of boots

squealing the ice that has no choice but
to give in and split, when the wind itself

remembers being wordless and clean.

Where Did You Go?

I went thin as pears, all sliced-up and see-through. I went halfway to happy. I went to a place where I don't have to answer. I went sniff in the air. I went to the arms of another. I went bent as bones. I went to a job without a computer, where I stand in a field and the sun wets my back. I went behind the numbers on a wristwatch. I went hundreds of miles from your eyes. I went all unmarriage and you cannot stop me. I went where your questions stop smack in the air and long before they can get to my ears. I went to before I even know you. That spot in the morning about to begin, that curl of a mouth turning into a smile, that moment a flower opens up like a hand.

Things

My life is filled with things. Red things, square things. Things I sit on. Things to help me eat. Things are everywhere and since they are, I can't escape them. One time I tried. Tried giving up things for an hour. Said to myself, *don't look, don't touch*. I tried turning myself into air, a breeze, a waft across a lavender room. When that didn't work, because how could it, I realized the things had won. Only one way to go. I had to become a thing. I sat down on my sofa-thing. I called out some words, which are also a thing. Told the world to come get me, use me to scrape a potato, use me to paint a wall. Do whatever it takes to make the want of me grow in your eyes. For me to be the thing you need.

Speck

Started smaller than salt, we did. One cell, two. Took a while until there were roads and condos and bombs. Yes, it took billions of years, but year-billions move slower than people-billions. Think of the noise-splash of what would be human being stepping its foot-thing onto land for the first time. Compare that to the thud of fireworks to start off the new year as if that's how long we have lived.

Each of us starts off a speck. Egg and sperm spin into billions of cells, then comes the slap as we leave our mother-ocean and enter the billions of seconds in an average-sized life. How we break down speck by speck. Until death becomes our mother, birthing our bodies into the ground, or our ashes into the sea -- the sea that strokes the shore like a hand reaching for something it once lost.

Parking Lots are Where They Keep the Sheep Now

After the cold stopped being cold. After we had to stop burning things. Burning anything. After we gave up our cars. After the sheep wandered into the town looking for food that wasn't hard as pearls. After we tried to eat the sheep but cooking got too hot and we were not strong enough to pull apart the sinew. After we looked at one another seven billion times and said it's you, no no, it's you. After we didn't even need the wool because we didn't need sweaters and also we could cut off our own hair to knit sweaters with if that were ever necessary. After we pushed the leftover shells of cars down to the dry patch where the lake used to be, and left them to rust or die or whatever it is cars do. After the sheep kept banging their noses against the windscreens because maybe they thought we had coldness or food when we didn't have either. After we roped them together and walked them down to the parking lots with the open storefronts that were gaping like mouths that can't scream anymore. After we left the sheep and never spoke of them again. After we became after.

Definition

This little boy asks his family what a lemon is. The mother, mostly apron, says oh I use it in my cooking. Also to sprinkle on fish. The father, who is rumpled like the evening paper, says, Ha! A lemon is the car your mother's brother sold me. The boy's older sister is mostly boy-drunk and says she uses lemons to bleach freckles off her face and also to blonde up her hair. Then the boy asks his grandmother what a lemon is. She is round-shouldered and pucker-skinned. She only comes downstairs once a day. Otherwise she stays in the attic, where she lives. A tiny window, a tinier view. *The sun is a lemon*, she says. *Sometimes a slice, sometimes a wedge. It fits different each day in my window she says. Each day it's a little less yellow that it was the day before.*

When You Lift Up

the ocean skin, standing on the sand shore like you are, finding the exact place in the waterlip, you see the fishes, not swimming, not oozing the blue like you thought but instead they are having tea, and all in one giant head turn, they look at you, exclamation straightening their bodies. *Go away!* They say in one together voice. *We will call you if we need you.*

When you lift up the earth skin, standing on the pavement like you are, finding the exact place in the dirtlip, you see that it's not all rock bog like you thought but rather rose roots and tree toes dug in and stretching, stretching. And all in one giant leg turn, they aim at you, comma curling them into one giant together kick. *Go away!* They seem to say. *We will call you if we need you.*

When you lift up your life skin, standing in the past and future like you are, you find the exact place on the calendar lip where you see your memories, your dreams and it's not all dark hearts and feather dreams like you thought, but rather a day parade, a tango. Turning and dipping, all of it looping into one giant ampersand saying your life is AND and AND and AND. *Come here*, the days of your life say in one together voice, *we are calling.*

When You Come Back, Then Maybe I Can Leave

1. A house is a. It is not a verb. If you never heard the word out loud, you'd say it wrong. (See love.) A house is taller than you. It has walls that are thicker than you. At night, it gets darker than you. (See doubt.)

2. A house is a. It is not a noun. It is a container inside other containers, and it holds containers, too. It holds people with bodies and hearts. (See eggshell.) It's inside a neighborhood, a town, a world. (See inside and inside and inside.)

3. A house is a. I thought you were one. I thought love was one. I was going to buy a shelf. I was going to buy a dinner plate. (See trying to plant a dolphin.)

Your House

The street lamps, their hunched necks bowed in prayer, your car rust metal-red, dark as old blood, the porch with its raggedy wicker chair where your grandfather sat for hours, the morning paper petaled into a flower at his feet. The smell of browning grass, musky and damp and overgrown. They sky since you left me, a bulge of rain, a cotton of clouds filled with the air they forgot to exhale.

Power Out

The whole city blackens. Like a chicken. Like a fish. You thump around the apartment-box, bump into the bed-box. All in search of a flashlight. No bars on your fancy, fancy phone. You dig out a transistor radio. It was your mother's and she thought you might need it someday. That was before she died, even though you might need her someday. The transistor croaks and hisses, here and there, spits out a word. Like Grid. Or citywide. And the dark is getting darker. You remember that your phone has a flashlight, but now you are thinking of how long you have survived without your mother. How long you can live without light. You take a seat to wait it out.

The Man, Not Like the Fish

couldn't swim. Went down a third, gurgly time. The water, not like his bedquilt at home, was freezing and didn't know him. The wife, not like the trees, ran towards the water, her screamy arms waving, not like the branches that were brittle and snap. The hole in the rowboat, not like the hole in their marriage which was gaping and constant, was covered by a mat of wet leaves. Their argument moments before and him rowing solo to the middle of the lake, was sudden, not like the seep of water that soaked his foot, the boat dropping out from under him. The fish, not like the man whose eyes were bulging now fishlike, had nothing but the water to hold him up.

Woman/Bird

Woman walks the bird she caught one day in a weeping tree. The bird now tied to a string above her not five feet long. Just long enough to skim the sky. Her pet, she tells her friends. But really, she wants the bird to catch the dreams she had that flew away. *Bring them to me*, the woman says. *You are lucky*, she tells the bird, *you have the gift of flight. If it were me, I'd bathe myself all day in the gauze of clouds, fill the air with stretch and song so loud no one would forget I was here.*

Bird walks the woman he caught one day as he waited in a willow tree. Keeps her on a string below him not five feet long. Tells his bird friends she is his human. But really, he is safe now from the scavenge of vultures, the zigzag of lightning on a summer night. The bird is held by the gravity of flight, always having to skitter away at the slightest sound, the clouds not strong enough to rest on. *You are lucky*, he wants to tell the woman. *You have the gift of land, If I had the pull of earth wanting to always keep me, the heft of a foot, big enough to leave a print, a hollow, I'd bathe myself all day in the swim of mud, push dirt together enough to start a mountain so high no one would forget I was here.*

Nightstreet.

Umbrella Man bobbling down the cobblestones. Dark jacket and hat under a shower of rainstars. Makes me think of you and the last time I saw you. The low rumble of love that used to be, that we tried and tried to get back. Me always thinking – this time will be different. But different never came. Me always thinking *If only the sun, if only the sun.* But the sun was ages and ages ago. Long before me standing here alone tonight watching this stranger walking down the street. Before the haze of the lamplight, gauzy and fog. Before his reflection on the rain-soaked stones Then his shadow. Then his ghost.

Home Shopping

Late night, all alone. Amethyst twinkling from the TV set. The beautiful "o" of stones. I feel like an "o" myself, a zero, because 3 AM is when the world gets so quiet, you hear everything. The host is a piano of teeth and a candle of eyes. She says things like *special value, very rare*, and I'm thinking she doesn't mean me. No, she is talking about the necklace. Every stone faceted, perfect. She flickers it under the camera lights and the amethyst looks like nightstars which takes me back to my own summer nights, on a blanket with some boyfriend or other, the smell of sweetgrass and his ropey, teenaged neck. His hands damp, a tremble of lust and even the sky wasn't bigger than we were. I look back at the TV. I wonder if amethyst has a smell.

We Aren't Broken Yet

But we are eggshell. Our world is marble, laminate. We roll and roll on the countertop. A tap against it and we crack. Have you ever heard of a cupped palm, a cradle? This is the myth our ancestors passed down before they themselves broke into bits. Sometimes we hear of one that doesn't even care. Paints eyes on itself and climbs up a wall. And all we ever hear after is the shattering. We don't hear anything after that.

The Smoke Trees

They began as acorn knots on the lawn-moss. Then they smelled like damp wood after a good hard rain. Then their shells flecked and splintered, and they began to grow. They held our childhood in each little finger-branch, their hair grew wild with leaves, and we watched them grow. We sat for whole summers at a time with smoke trees curling in the wind, leaning the way they do, their arms letting go of us, sending us into the world. Finally, the smoke trees were fire and love and how everything, everything passes. We sat in the ashy air breathing all of it in.

There Was a Time

when you knew night was coming and not by the numerals on your watch, not by some tick-tock time step you danced like a marionette. No, you knew night was coming by the bubbles starting up in the air, the sniff of everything possible, and you were all it needed to begin.

There was a time when smoke was perfume that wafted off a living fire and not from ashes swept in a pile, and you'd get dressed, sparkle your hair, and red up your lips. You knew that somewhere out there, there was a boy with a kiss waiting on his mouth. You knew there was a space in the air right next to him waiting for you to fill. Dayflowers all around were dimming themselves, giving up to the darkening blend of twilight and music and love.

This was the time when there wasn't time. No second hand creeping along, swooping in like a dark bird forcing you back inside the house. You lived, and you lived well with no one to tell you that you were early or late and you never were either. Everything that happened fit you like a gown made just for you, nipped in and perfect at the waist.

Lone Earring

Found last night in my jewelry box. Cheap dangle of rhinestone. Clip on and just a bit of a pinch. I wore the pair of them that night we drove around and drove around, the two of us new and hungry for us. We found a quiet spot to park. The city all around us. The beep and roar of living cars and the island of us two in the middle. You kissed my earring right off that night, I would later joke. Later you found it on the mat, hung it on the rearview, attached it to your college tassel, and liked to watch it sway as you drove along. Liked how it shimmered in the sun, the glassy stab of it that probably still hurt a little even after we were done.

Motherfather

My mother became both. After the father part left
us one night, walked out into the rain, left
footprints on the spring grass that dried up
by morning and blew away. *Motherfather* went
to work. Got a job at the Five & Dime, where they
let her take home leftover stuff, the stuff that wouldn't
sell. Chipped ceramic ashtrays, a lidless saucepan
she would use to fry up cheap hamburger
seasoned with too much salt.

My brother didn't take it well. Told *motherfather* to put
a plate for my father at the head of the table. Then,
he pushed his own plate away like all of her excuses.
Later, she'd try to tuck him in, but he'd ask for dad,
blame her for chasing him away with her plainness
and her love of routine. *Motherfather* tried to do boy things

with him, anything to fill in the father space. Brought home
toys from the store they were throwing out for newer models.
Tiny soldiers he would line up and name the general after
my father, cap guns he'd load up and point at the world.

Landscape with Mother

Bills piled on the dining room table
and my mother with her head bent
under a bouffant of hair. Some might
think it's worry that's weighing her down,
that if not for the cost of living, my mother

would sprout wings, maybe soar across
a field where home and food and electric
were rich brown soil and berries and stars.
Some might say she could fly low
onto a jagged rock that juts up to meet her,
shapes itself to what she needs, the wildflowers
that grow in the tiny cracks

reaching up in surrender, in prayer.

Other Histories

Not the one you always tell
where you grew up wrong, but wised
your way out. Not the romance history
where you shake your head about divorce
and nightmare dates. Not even your medical
history blurry with cigarette smoke
and clogged with red meat.

But that other history, that private
history someone would have to dig
for, deep in the deep, even if it felt
to them like spooning their way
to the center of the earth. That history
where you held your mother's hand
that one last time as it went weightless
with her death. That history of your father's
mountain self on the sofa for most of your
teenaged life. That history of one day
after another until all of a sudden,

random catch in the morning mirror
and where did your younger self go?
Taken somehow by that sneaky sway
of pendulum time, that sway that takes
pretty and turns it into *good for her age*,
sways back again to the earthbed holding
one friend, and then another. That history
filled with calls you didn't make, trips
you didn't go on. That history, ticking
back and forth and forth and back,
past into future, future into past.

Wherein I Watch My Uncle at Thanksgiving Sit in My Dead Father's Favorite Chair

Focus on the TV, I am thinking, but that's how the trouble
starts. A program about the year so far -- riots and looting
and my uncle harrumphing how this country has its ass in a sling.
We watch the shimmy of fire and flying glass. Instead of smoke,
we get the aroma of a turkey, same as last year. Same as every year
since I was a kid. I can still feel the stomach spin of my uncle lifting
me in the air above his head, and me an airplane. My father would
be sitting in his favorite chair, nervous until my uncle landed me
safely. Then we'd go in to eat.

Now, my uncle sits in my father's chair. My father's chair
empty ten years now. Heart attack from working so hard.
Chump, my uncle called him to my mother, *getting jobs
for those animals, feeding their unwanted brats*. My mother's
brother and so *we have to be nice*, she would say. *He's blood*,
she would say. Right now, I am a totter away from falling
off the fence I have always had to sit on. And when he starts
to doze off, *wake me when it's dinner*, something in me snaps

like a turkey wishbone, that favorite part of Thanksgiving,
me and my father, our elbows on the table and him letting
me get the bigger half. I'm thinking now what would
his wish be, so I jostle my uncle's shoulder. *Yes, he's blood*,
I think, *but so was my father*. My mother standing

in the dining room, bowl of broccoli in her hand.
Her mouth about to say something about family.
My uncle shaking the near-sleep off of him.
When I tell him "get up, this is my father's chair,"
my uncle stands up like a statue I'm about to tear
down. My father's ghost waiting to finally sit.

Seven Billion Later

And no one thought to bring enough food. My mother
would have shuddered scrolling the internet, the far-off

countries that include even ours. You have to be ready,
my mother would say, even if it means sharing what's yours.

She was always the one to take the burnt lamb chop,
the broken heel of bread. She'd sit at supper, head down,

eyes sneaking peaks at us enjoying it all and *that* was her food.
I remember family vacations, Long clamory drives, my mother

in the front seat doling out goldfish crackers from a baggie
because she understood the fidget of hunger. Once we were settled

with too much chew in our mouths to fight anymore, she'd turn back
around, having given my father the peace and quiet he needed to drive.

Then she would stare out the window, staring at the fields and fields,
the empty earth-table waiting for its invisible mother to take the wheel.

Death Sends Me an Email

This was the year I was going to be young, walk
the hell out of myself, unzip my skinsuit and Tinkerbell
the globe. *I really don't have time for death*, I say to
my computer and send Death's email to the trash.
Besides if it's important, Death can always text.
Or better yet, call. The way my sister called that last
time, though I didn't pick up the phone. No way to know
it was the last chance I'd have. But see, Death is that kind
of asshole, lurking behind curtains and jumping out – *surprise!*
Other times winking and winking the way he did my mother's
last agony year. No way to know what's on Death's fickle
mind, and so I fish out the email and open it. Turns out to be
spam from a window company -- *Death to bad insulation-*
in the subject line and I just misread. I sigh and settle back.
I can be young some other time. Travel some other year.
And then, I think of Death sitting at his own computer,
clearing out the backlog. I can only hope my name is in
some kind of file marked *get to this later*, the kind of email
he'd fuss over the wording, fidget every comma, maybe
show it to his wife for feedback, rewrite it a couple
of hundred times before he presses *send*.

Username

I forgot this one. The password, too. Online shoe store
I only needed once. Not like those other usernames

I used for a bit longer, *daughter, girlfriend, wife.*
My mother gave me a username the day I was born but

how many times did I forget? That night I sank
into high-school Kevin's leather jacket, smell of danger

and cool. How he told me I wasn't his girlfriend.
How I slept with him anyway. How years later,

my husband fessed up about motel charges
on our credit card. How I stayed with him

anyway. Maybe those times, I reset my username
because I was going to be a whole new person. A person

who needed online shoes. That's probably why I opened
the account. Bought a pair of shoes I never even wore,

wrong color, too small. But maybe this time.
who knows? Maybe I *would* go hiking if I had

the right pair of boots. I try to remember who I was
when I made up the username for this account. *Adventuregirl?*

Powerchick? Or maybe I went with the truth? I think
how every day, people around me or on the evening news

are putting their usernames on hospital charts, on grave markers.
I think back to my mother, last time I ever saw her, had no idea

what her own username was but still she was putting red lipstick on.
The nurse's aide stood next to her repeating my mother's username

careful and loud. My mother stared into a pocket mirror, at the lips
of a stranger pouting back. Locked, forever, out of the rest of her life

When Supper Was a Thing

Not dinner, but 6 o'clock supper.
My mother, faint sweat on her forehead,
but alive with a whole other life. I couldn't
imagine how the apron tied around her waist
was like the arms of her secret lover. I knew
nothing about boys. Or men. It's as if childhood
was saying *eyes front*. I was only eleven
and there was time for all that drama,
and that I should enjoy these last moments
before the rolling boil of adolescence set in.
Before I would look at my father as a robbed
man who would stoop over, heart attack very soon
and never know where my mother slipped off
to on Thursday nights. Or how supper was full
of tricks, salt giving everything flavor, food dye
making everything pretty, our family sitting
at the table, everyone sharing the same meal.

To My Relatives Who Died Before COVID

My father who loved the distance. Loved being far from things. From us.

My other-city sister, who slumped sudden over a flip phone and wasn't able to mute.

My mother, always lipstick, always powder. A mask would not have stopped her, *because*, she'd say, *people know.*

My grandmother, flu of '18, who knitted and baked and ended up with vision loss and hearing loss and that was her shelter in place.

My free-spirit aunt, who wouldn't have stayed home nohow and rather she'd slip out to one of those bars with takeout only, her in the alley with her son's best friend, the two of them not hearing my uncle's muffled footsteps.

All of them not believing. *We didn't see it coming. It can't happen.*

And yet I remember the time we all stood on the beach and looked at the horizon. We thought it swallowed everything.

Look! someone said. *A whole boat hidden behind my thumb!*

The Never of Us

Quiver of first light and the blip of alarms,
today will be better, today will be better.

We hope for enough milk to cover our cereal,
for the greed of the moon to be pushed back

into the sky. Somehow, we know that the earth
has started its slow rid of us. Earthquakes and fires

and all of that. All of that rain. We catch our train,
we meet for drinks. We joke that the rumble beneath

our feet is part of getting older. Every so often our child-
selves poke through, keep us sleepless -- or wish us

back to birth, or forward to the after of us, or to the never of us
which hangs above, a safe and faraway star.

Once, You Were Earth

You felt every lick of wind
as it formed your mountains,
the breathless scoop of your valleys.
Maybe you sighed and said that's life.
Some days plant a tree while other days
kill them. One day you decided that
you weren't earth, after all, didn't want
the thud of every footstep walking
on your life. So you burned and quaked
the way our big earth is doing. Trying
to make yourself an unspoken planet
one with all its histories locked
in museums. Your own museum
being memory.

The Moon Takes the E Train

Stumbles drunk from a downtown dive, swirling himself *milkintocoffee* down the stairs and onto the train and then forgets his way home, gets off instead at Forty-Deuce, looks around and remembers the old-style scene, hookers and pornflix, how often in his fullness he would push some poor sucker into *Mr. Nasty's* peepshow, watch him skulk out later, face wiped off, slither home to *bridgeandtunnel*, lighter twenty bucks, but then the whole place went carnival, wax museums and kiddy theatre, life-sized Elmo and Elsa who will pose with you for a hefty tip, and he's looking around at all the lights blinking into the darkened dark, and that's when a couple approaches the moon and asks to take a selfie, how much it would mean what with the moon being the thing that made them fall in love, and the moon has heard this all before, how he's pulled the tides, and planted romance, but really, he has a long, long night ahead, trying to remember which subway will take him back to the sky, but instead, the moon takes a breath, looks at his reflection in the couple's eyes, nestles in between them and smiles.

Pizza Hut, 1990

Outside, the rainstutter.
Inside, garlic waft, chatter
of highchair kids. The waitress
staccato, you tapping your fingers.
Say it, I say to rain outside, my
voice bouncing back off the tinted
window glass. The stop of the drops,
the start again. Just fall, I tell it,
just come in one steady stream,
like a river, like Mountain Dew
fizzing out of a soda machine.
Like a man who doesn't love me
anymore.

The Sun is as Hot as a Simile

Not just any simile. Not the supermodel
smoke-eye or a sizzle pan on the breakfast
stove. No. This sun is hotter than that. Hotter
than Miles or Trane playing slidebone down
the spine. Hotter than stammer or collar-tug
or lust. Hotter even than the letters for hot,
sticking humid to each other, the h seated
and nervous, the o with its open mouth,
and the t, arms welcoming with waiting
embrace. Truth is, this sun is less *like* you
and much more *as* you. Becoming a single
hum, notes that singe the helpless blue,
turn into flame and burn itself circle
into the sky, curl up yellow and shine.

When Charley Says Goodbye

His words hit rat-a-tat at my heart.
I can write him into the biography
of want that started in the third grade
when David R. did not return my
valentine, how I saw it later curled
up on the floor next to the trash.
Back then, there was always Dion
on the radio, that turned later into
the Beatles, that turned into the Who.
Album to cassette to CD, but funny
how hurt never grew up, never went
adult, easy listening and background.
How when I look straight at Charley,
I can't help but also see David R.,
my heart still a valentine, hurt-riddled
and curled. Also funny how if Charley
were to turn himself backwards, the way
we played the album in reverse to find
proof that Paul was dead, or if Charley
were to turn back time like that, tell
me he's sorry, he didn't mean it,
I would most likely believe.

The Night

      All perch and blackbird,
the window that's always closed,

      the air outside tapping
to come in, your dreams inside tapping

      to fly out. If someone were
to slash you open, you would likely bleed

      stars. If you were to slash
yourself open, you would lie down,

      believing your own death.
All the time, stars scattered on the floor

      beneath the window,
blackbird, beat, tap.

Supermarket, 11 AM

Cruising the cereal aisle, burst of corn pops
and leprechauns winking at me, the way
summer boys winked at me all those years ago.
Friday nights at the *Left Bank Lounge*, glass clink
and a local band covering Phil Collins, smack of
English Leather in the air. And then those awful
mornings after where I was left broken, put back
together but never completely whole.

Now, I am older and oh so wise, at least that's
what I tell the morning mirror. I walk down
the cereal aisle, some long-gone song tinkles
out of an overhead speaker, and it all comes back,
each box cologned with everything that some
focus group thought would speak to the hungry hearts
of middle-aged women, women who are still
wheeling their girliness around in a shopping cart.

I scan this wall of oat clusters and honey nuts
from top to floor, pick up a box, examine
calories per serving, total carbs, and realize
this is more than I ever thought about when
choosing a boy to take home. Back then,
I only needed the thrum of a band, guitar
strum and cymbal crash, *Johnny and the
Nevergreens*, that was enough to lullaby me
into my next casual fling. Nothing at all like
picking up a box of corn flakes, shaking it to
test the weight, checking the expiration date,
to see how long, if at all, it will last.

Racing

I'm a young girl these days, though
no one would know, my age being higher
on the inside. Another funeral just blew
by my nose. High school friend. I watched
her being lowered into the ground
but chose not to smell it, didn't want
Inside Me to know. Instead, I went
home and called the hair salon -- *blacken
my roots, dark my hair low.* Then I stood
back to watch myself from the stands,
the daily race I run. Myself with myself.
Both Me's rounding another turn. Inside Me,
surprisingly fast, given her love of an afternoon nap.
Outside Me, slowing of course, what with the heels
she insists I wear. Both Me's knowing what lies ahead.
Both wanting to be the Me that crosses the finish
line, both wanting to be the Me that feels that
cut of cool air, that final slice of victory flag,
as it's waving me in.

Real Supper

The mother of my teen-aged years was always
on a diet. *Metra-cal*, vibrating belts, original
Weight Watcher meetings in a basement.

She wore flowered dusters and gray polyester pants.
She looked 60 at 38. *The first thing a man notices,*
she would tell me, *is your figure.* She would grill

sad white fish fillets and serve the rest of us *Hamburger Helper.*
My father pushed it away, saying he wanted real supper,
like the kind they have on TV.

Next night, another diet was over and we were eating
pot roast, cups of chocolate pudding. *What a man wants,*
my father would tell me, *is comfort.* He told me my mother

is beautiful, though I wondered if he ever said it to her.
The last time I saw my father, he was in the hospital,
tubed up and vented, life support after a stroke.

My mother sitting beside him after visiting hours,
because the doctor told us this would be his last night.
Her, so happy that my father squeezed back, the doctor

telling her that means he heard you, and me standing
there wondering if she was thinking, *well, it's about time.*

That Year, the Snow

and us, cottonpacked in mittens and scarves.
The river we had been living had stopped.
All the boats frozen in place.

We didn't worry about our own weight
and how it should have groaned the ice.
We wouldn't have listened anyway.

Noon was chiming from a faraway clock.
Our mothers calling lunch. Under all the ice
and snow, the hard pack of land that, like us,

would soften with time and were we to stand
right there and never move, by spring
we would be up to our shoulders in mud.

Every Year, Old Gets Older

Once, I sat in a classroom, ninth grade algebra,
and rather than X, I filled my head with boys

and the specific formulas it would take to get
David A. to ask me out again. Or I thought about

Joey D., who liked me, but also liked my best friend, Jill.
And then there was Greg T., leather jacket and everyone's

swoon. The other day I was mixing cake batter, laughed
to myself about the algebra my teacher said I would need

at just this moment. How to cut a recipe in case of divorce,
though I'm sure that's not what he meant. Even though

that's what happened, and how now I am thinking
again about formulas – good years and how many

are left. What are the most youthful haircuts, and am
I too old for cat-eye. How I have to go back to looking at boys

only this time calling them men. On TV, I am watching
a 100 year-old-woman who has race-walked her way

onto the evening news. The reporter in visible awe.
I begin doing the math in my head, how many good years

as I look at this woman who has added to the recipe
which at this point in my life, I was thinking

was just about subtraction. The reporter asks her
what's the secret? How did you finish a race

with so many younger competitors. She looks
at him like he's a math problem, like she's

figuring out how someone asks a question like this.
"I put one foot in front of the other," she says,

not a trace of anything in her voice, "and then,
I do it again."

The Heart: a Definition

It beats. It tells you
who and who not
to love. It tick tocks
your body, easing you
further and further away
from your birth. It's a
valentine, cut out and
velvet, and it's filled up
with chocolate. It doesn't
stop until you die. It is
etched on the bark of a tree.
The heart is the acorn inside
the tree you turned into. It is
a queen in the country of
a deck of cards. It breaks.
It will break again. It is
already broken.

There We Were, Pinned

underneath our own bodies. What
can you do when you've just been mugged
by lust? Sure, we knew better, knew
what liars the moon and tequila could be,
still we couldn't resist. Besides, in that
low, achy light, it was easy to stretch
possibility, to see the sweat on your back
glisten into some ancient, holy river.
I began to sing the truth of a hummingbird,
you tried to push a lifetime inside me.
Then we began to rise, even growing wings.
We flirted by cloud puffs, sipped on cups
of starlight. And when it was over, we
slammed back to Earth into this bed of
cement, with our bodies outlined in chalk.
Slowly eased what was left of ourselves
out from under the dead hulk flesh
we would crawl back into again
and again, pull on, arm by arm
like a nettled sweater we wear out
of habit, but tear off whenever
the moment is right.

Our Star

is really the sun, and billions of miles
away, maybe someone is wishing on it,
wishing for a last desperate chance at love.
But here I am, on this beach where people
stretch out like dead exclamation points,
tanning themselves to our star. Nearby,
a wave breaks. Pebble and salt and soapy
foam. I wonder how far that wave could
have gone without the beach to stop it?
I pick up a grain of sand, infinitesimal,
but this is how our star might look to that
billion-mile lover. I picture him a human
wave, aching to break past his own beach-locked
future, finally able to get whatever he could
wish for on some distant pin of light.

ACKNOWLEDGMENTS

"Map of Me," *Pedestal*

"What I Would Tell Adam and Eve," *Edison Literary Review*

"First Conversation, Maybe," *Mid-American Review*

"Our Shadows Met Before We Did," *Stonecoast*

"How the Light Hits," *Potomac Review*

"If I Turn Animal," *Pithead Chapel*

"Go On, Count Your Chickens," *Misfit*

"The River's Wife," *Schuykill Valley Journal*

"Careful," *Concho River Review*

"When I Think About Jake," *K'in*

"The Year of You Gone," *Gargoyle*

"Other Summers," *Main Street Rag*

"The Marsh Fills Up," *Thimble Lit*

"The Better Way to Go," *Misfit*

"It is 1951," *Naugatuck River Review*

"Picasso's Weeping Woman," *Misfit*

"Shopping for the Storm," *I-70 Review*

"Direction," *Maryland Literary Review*

"The First Snow," *New York Quarterly*

"*Where Did You Go?*" *Unbroken Journal* and *Mackinaw Review*

"Things," *January Review*

"Parking Lots are Where They Keep the Sheep Now," *January Review* and *Mackinaw Review*

"Definition," *Pedastal* and *Mackinaw Review*

"When You Come Back, Maybe Then I Can Leave," *Pacifica Literary Review*

"Your House," *Goats Milk* and *Shot Glass*

"Power Out," *Ginosko*

"The Man, Not Like the Fish," *New York Quarterly*

"Woman/Bird," *Unbroken Journal*

"Nightstreet," *Shot Glass*

"Home Shopping," *Unbroken Journal* and *Mackinaw Review*

"There Was a Time," *Michigan Quarterly Review*

"Lone Earring," *Unbroken Journal* and *Mackinaw Review*

"Motherfather," *San Pedro River Review*

"Landscape with Mother," *Home Planet News*

"Other Histories," *Midwest Quarterly*

"Wherein I Watch my Uncle," *Roanoke Review*

"Seven Billion Later," *Maintenant*
"Death Sends Me an Email," *Concho River Review*
"Username," *Misfit*
"When Supper Was a Thing," *Valparaiso Poetry Review* and *Gasconade*
"To My Relatives Who Died Before COVID," *Boston Literary Review* and *Gasconade*
"The Never of Us," *Poetica Review*
"Once, You Were Earth," *Main Street Rag*
"The Moon Takes the E Train," *NYC FROM THE INSIDE*
"Pizza Hut, 1990," *One Art*
"The Night," *I-70 Review*
"Racing," *Main Street Rag*
"Real Supper," *Concho River Review*
"That Year, the Snow," *Long Islander*
"Every Year, Old Gets Older," *The Macguffin*
"The Heart: a Definition," *Brevitas*
"There We Were, Pinned," *Saranac Review*

A special thank you to George Wallace for his editorial help on the manuscript.

Also George Wallace, Jennifer Juneau, and Sarah Freligh, three of my favorite poets for their generous blurbs.

And to the writing community, both online and in-person, for their ongoing support.

And, of course, to Gloria Mindock and everyone at Červená Barva Press for believing in my work.

ABOUT THE AUTHOR

Francine Witte is an award-winning poet, flash fiction writer, and playwright. She is the author of 12 books of poetry and flash fiction and her work has appeared in numerous journals and anthologies. She is a native New Yorker and attends and produces poetry events in the vibrant NYC scene. She is the co-host and co-curator of the online reading, *The Prose Garden*. She is the flash fiction editor for FLASH BOULEVARD and *South Florida Poetry Journal*. A former high school English teacher, she now leads writing prompt sessions on zoom. Witte holds an MFA in Creative Writing/Poetry from Vermont College and an MA from SUNY Binghamton. Visit her website at francinewitte.com.